The Checklist Mindset

(For Entrepreneurs, Employees & Action-Takers)

Automate & Scale Your Small Business or 9-5 Job into an Appointment-Based Machine

By Robert Plank
www.DoubleAgentMarketing.com

All rights reserved. No part of this publication may be reproduced or transmitted in any form or by any means, electronic or mechanical, including photocopy, recording or any information storage and retrieval system, without prior permission in writing from the publisher.

© 2017 by Robert Plank, (408) 277-0904

Chapter 1: Peak Productivity and a Winning Mindset	2
Chapter 2: Google Tools (Gmail, Google Calendar, Google Drive)	9
Chapter 3: Templates & Canned Responses	19
Chapter 4: Follow-Through & Complete Everything You Start	25
Chapter 5: Help Desk & Operations Manual (ZenDesk)	35
Chapter 6: Appointment Scheduler (Calendly)	46
Chapter 7: Automation Triggers (Zapier)	53
About Robert Plank	62
Thanks for Supporting the Book	64

Chapter 1: Peak Productivity and a Winning Mindset

Please understand why you're doing what you're doing. Whether you're a self-employed entrepreneur running your own company or you're an hourly employee working for someone else, you need to know what your goals are, what you're doing day to day, and what you should be doing at this exact second.

Many of the usual clichés you hear about "being productive" or "getting more done in less time" simply don't work! People tell you to create a to-do list of 100 tasks, prioritize them, and chip away a little bit at a time. I don't know about you, but that sounds very demotivating and demoralizing to me. If you're stressed, overwhelmed, and you feel like you're always running out of time, you need to do a few things to change what you're doing day to day in whatever office tasks you have going on. Simplify things, and avoid that to-do list to also avoid burnout.

Four Daily Tasks Explained

Here's a better way: Four Daily Tasks! In whatever job you find yourself in, focus on the four most important things every day. You don't work eight hours in a day. In fact, if you find yourself always overwhelmed, you might even be working fifteen minutes or less. I've found that four is the magic number. Every day, in whatever computer-related tasks I'm performing, I'll knock out one quick 10-minute task, another 45-minute task, a third 45-minute task, and finally a fourth 45-minute task.

This totals up to 2 hours and 25 minutes of productivity every day. Space this out in an eight-hour workday. Account for mid-morning breaks, lunch breaks, leaving early, and wasting time. Your end result: 2 hours and 25 minutes of pure focused energy during the day. This works better than struggling for eight to twelve hours. It's a better alternative than the dreaded "all-nighter." Some tasks can wait several days. Not every task is urgent, and by using Four Daily Tasks, you'll fit actions into these 10-minute and 45-minute windows. You can chunk up or "batch up" small actions into focused sessions. Those tiny two-minute, five-minute, and eight-minute tasks that were bothering you are completed one fell swoop.

The Three-Day Window

Any enthusiasm for a new project dies off in three days. If you have an important work assignment, or if you're running your own business, and you have an idea for that next landing page, website, webinar, video, or product, do it now. Take your best first-draft stab at it, and clean up the pieces later.

The three-day window: if you have an idea for something on Monday morning, you have until Thursday morning to finish it. Don't make it perfect. That's a first draft you can improve later.

If you have real deadlines, you'll get a better handle on what you can accomplish in a given day or week, especially if you're focused and if you cut out the noise. Become more organized. "Organized" sounds like items fit into convenient cubbyholes, as if a gigantic system has taken over your life. Many times, "to-do list" based productivity ADDS time to your day. Managing the system takes longer than the time you would have saved simplifying your life. I believe in stripping away the nonsense and making things simple. Four daily tasks, have a three-day window for projects, have deadlines for those milestones, and accomplish them.

Associate, or anchor, this positive action. Get used to meeting goals, and you can reward yourself for a job well done.

Timer + Accountability = Focus

Don't get distracted. When you're in your focused flow state, shut off all distractions: your phone, instant messenger, Facebook, email, everything, and focus on one 45-minute milestone that you can complete in a single sitting. This might mean writing a shorter blog post that only takes 45 minutes to complete.

Get on the phone and talk to that important coaching client or customer for 45 minutes. After you complete that single 45-minute task, get off the computer. If possible, go outside and take a walk. If you're in an office environment, shut off your computer monitor, or change your focus to something more paper-based or desk-based. That way, you're not switching gears so much. You avoid distraction. More importantly and more long-term, you break the cycle of addiction to distraction.

A few tools are helpful in this situation. Number one, a countdown timer. Open a web browser tab, go to Google.com, and type "countdown timer." Set the timer to ten minutes, or forty-five minutes, and let the timer count down while you knock out that task. You'll feel some anxiety as the timer counts down. You'll close those unimportant browser tabs and notifications. You'll focus on finishing that task before the timer is done.

Next, an accountability partner. At the beginning of the day, think of those four tasks you'll complete: 10-minute, 45-minute, 45-minute, 45-minute. Send anyone you know (coworker, friend, or family member) an email or text quickly listing those four items you're about to begin AND complete. Then, at the end of the day, send them another text, listing which of those four tasks you accomplished, and which ones you didn't accomplish. For a great example of this Four Daily Tasks accountability system, go to FourDailyTasks.com/group and join it to see many other people like yourself posting their four tasks daily.

Sometimes, I'll record my screen using a tool such as Camtasia Recorder or the free web-based tool Screencast-O-Matic.com. I'll record a video showing those on-screen actions on my computer. For whatever reason, when those cameras roll, I get the feeling as if someone is looking over my shoulder. I'm not going to record myself opening email or Facebook. I'll record myself being productive and completing that task in a short spurt.

Stay Healthy and Active

Please keep your health in check. It doesn't make any sense to stay awake for three days straight, or to survive only on fast food because you're stressed or you're short on time. If you don't take care of both your mind and body, it will catch up to you. You might think you were super-productive last night because you never left your office chair, or you only slept two hours a night, but you eventually crashed. An even worse scenario: your productivity slowed and you didn't realize it.

Take care of yourself. Wake up early, get a good night's sleep, drink lots of water, take lots of walks (or runs or drives), and avoid busywork. Take care of yourself first and you'll get into a better mindset. This makes you more productive and you can plug into various tools to multiply your efforts. Remove daily "busywork" tasks from your everyday life and add automation to focus on fun activities that give you fulfillment and enjoyment. Accelerate your progress. Sit down at the computer, knock out a task, then get off the computer to enjoy what matters in life.

If you have a hobby, if you want to travel, if you want to spend more time with your family, you can do whatever you want. Just realize that work, productivity and office tasks are best done in quick, short spurts. Be in a super-focused mindset, sit down at that computer "hot-seat" and complete your tasks. If you don't think you have the time to answer emails, or run social media ads, or edit a book, carve out time for it. Plan ahead and give yourself a 45-minute chunk today or tomorrow. When that appointment comes up, take it seriously, meet with yourself, and knock out what needs to be done.

Important Notes

1. To-do lists don't work and aren't sustainable. Four Daily Tasks is a far better solution because it forces you to simplify your life, and chunk or batch up small tasks to avoid switching gears.

2. The Four Daily Task system is structured like this: complete an easy 10-minute task, then a 45-minute task, then another 45-minute task during the day, and finally, one last 45-minute task.

3. Install Screencast-O-Matic.com to record your computer screen. It helps you stay focused! Also consider a countdown timer and joining our Facebook group at FourDailyTasks.com/group.

Questions

1. What is the three-day window?

2. What is an accountability partner and how does it make you more productive?

3. Why is it important to rest, exercise, and eat well?

Chapter 2: Google Tools (Gmail, Google Calendar, Google Drive)

It no longer makes sense to write notes on paper, or even use desktop tools such as Microsoft Word. There's a better way. The old way was to use a word processor, type notes and sift through files and folders. You weren't always sure which files you had. In super ancient times, you might have saved files on floppy disks, USB sticks or shared network folders.

Google Cloud: Gmail, Calendar, Drive

The new way is to store it in the "cloud." Use your browser, computer, phone, or tablet to edit the same notes and files, and even share those files with others -- with "read only" or "read and write" permissions. With the cloud, it doesn't matter which device you use to jot down those quick notes. Read important text on your phone when you lay in a hammock, browse for something at the park on your tablet, or write something on your computer. Google provides free productivity tools that replace outdated solutions like Microsoft Word, Outlook, and Excel.

Google's free web-based email tool (Gmail) is far better than any other email client. This organizes your life and helps you schedule appointments.

You can see the agenda for your upcoming day with another web-based tool called Google Calendar.

Google Drive allows you to store files including images and video in the cloud, then access them from any computer in the world.

Drive has a built-in word processor called Google Docs. You can write documents (term papers, essays, reports) and share them with others. You might write one paragraph, and someone else can login on their own Google account, and they'll see you typing words in real time. They can edit or add. You can track changes, meaning you see which users made which changes.

Drive also contains a spreadsheet tool called Google Sheets, similar to Microsoft Excel. A spreadsheet is a grid with rows and columns. Use spreadsheets to create multi-part checklists to measure the results of your actions in your business or job. Log repetitive tasks and get a better handle on the payoff.

Gmail (Web-Based Email)

Access Gmail from any web browser, phone, or tablet. Gmail doesn't use folders. Instead, it uses labels and archives to manage messages.

An email comes to your inbox. This is a new message.

You can delete the message, or label that email as an "accounting" issue, a "receipt" email for something you purchased, or a "subscription" email for a newsletter. This helps you to differentiate between important and unimportant messages in your email inbox. Instead of filing things away in folders, add labels to emails.

One email can have multiple labels. You could have a receipt from a purchase that your accountant also needs to see, for example.

This is better than the old "Microsoft Outlook" system where you'd wait for messages to download. You would file them in folders, and backup your Outlook database somewhere. None of that exists anymore. It's all online.

It gets even better. Most people have an email inbox with at least 30,000 unread messages. They can't keep a handle on their email. They might clear it one time (inbox zero) but it quickly fills up again.

The solution: archive messages in Gmail. An email comes into your inbox, and you click and read it.

You could delete that message (send it to the trash) or you can "archive" it, which means it still exists, but it's hidden. Not in your inbox.

Your inbox contains new messages, much like a physical inbox of letters you might have on your desk. Archive a message, and it's no longer in your Inbox. It's filed away under an area of Gmail called All Mail. Click the "All Mail" link and you can see every email you've archived as well as the messages in your inbox. Your inbox becomes a short list of unread or read-but-unresolved messages you need to look at. In Gmail, you can search the entire All Mail section, and find any specific message.

Next, Conversations. Does this "old school" frustration with email sound familiar? An email message arrives. You reply to it. The other party replies back. Now you have multiple email messages that belong to the same thread. Gmail simplifies this and combines conversations together. (Many other web-based services and email clients have attempted to catch up to this simple innovation.) If an email arrives, reply to it right underneath that email, and when you get a reply back, that new message appears on the bottom.

This applies to forwards and email chains involving multiple people. Emails are now grouped together into conversations. You might have emailed back and forth with someone 20 or 50 times, but that is all combined into one discussion thread, much like a Skype or Facebook Messenger conversation.

Turn off notifications for emails (including Gmail), notifications on your phone, and your Chrome browser. Only check email a few times a day, and don't check email first thing in the morning. Gmail will change your life.

Google Calendar (Web-Based Calendar)

Google Calendar is a web-based (accessible from anywhere) calendar that shows your events (appointments) throughout the week. You can click on any time of day of any date -- today, in the past, or in the future, and schedule a block of time. If you need to remember an important meeting, call someone on the phone, or carve out time for yourself, use Google Calendar to set these appointments.

Warning: don't over-schedule yourself. Don't schedule sleep and bathroom breaks into your Google Calendar. (This sounds silly, but I've seen it.). Use it sparingly, so you'll notice when the 3-4 appointments of the day come your way.

You can access Google Calendar from any computer or web browser. Every modern smartphone or tablet (iPhone, Android, Samsung, Windows phone, etc.) has simple instructions to synchronize Google Calendar with your mobile device. This means you can set an appointment on your calendar from any web browser, and it appears on your phone.

It also works the other way. You can make an appointment on your phone when you're away from the office, and when you check that calendar at the computer, tablet, or laptop, that same appointment appears on every device.

You can have multiple calendars. For example, a calendar for yourself, a separate calendar for work activities, another for family activities, and they appear on the same screen labeled with different colors. You can share these "sub-calendars" with others, which means a few things. If your spouse wants to plan that family vacation to Disneyworld, he or she can add that to your "Family" calendar, but you don't want to share that information with coworkers, so they can't see that specific calendar, but your family members can.

If you want to show coworkers that you're busy (the time was blocked out) but they don't need to see what you've blocked out time for, you can do that (show only that you're "free" or "busy" as opposed to revealing my names or locations).

Share calendars with others and tell others they can add to that specific sub-calendar. You can give others access to see your blocked off time, but only show it as busy as opposed to showing the exact task. It's a powerful tool, especially when you use multiple sub-calendars. Create a sub-calendar for family, another for coworkers, one for business colleagues and partners (if that applies), and it all synchronizes to the web and the Cloud, and your devices.

I get an email from Google every morning saying, "Here are your appointments for today." When an important appointment is a few minutes away, Google emails me. A pop-up message appears on my browser, another pop-up on my phone, and another pop-up on my tablet. I have an upcoming appointment and I'm almost guaranteed to see the alert in one way or another. I'll have a good idea about how busy my day will be. Anyone I interact with, including friends, family, and coworkers, can see my availability.

Google Drive (Web-Based Backup & Storage)

Google Drive is Google's storage service, similar to Carbonite or Dropbox. They give you gigabytes of space that you can use to upload important Word documents, videos, graphics, or files to the cloud. You could backup your websites and your computer (family photos) to free up extra storage space.

You can create and share entire folders, or individual files (photos or documents). You can take an important picture on your phone, stash it on Google Drive, and pick it up on a computer or another device. You can edit a series of documents with someone else and stash them in the folder so you can collaborate.

Google Drive gets your files off the computer. You never know if that computer will get lost, stolen, or damaged. If you're an employee in a 9-5 job, ask your boss if this is allowed. Gmail For Work is an enterprise tool specifically for using these Cloud services in a business. Google Drive and everything we've discussed so far about the Cloud synchronizes to your mobile devices, and you can share them with others.

Google Docs (Word Processor)

Google Documents (or Google Docs) is an online document editing tool. Microsoft Word is a popular word processing tool to write reports or entire books. This is similar, but it exists online.

Open or create a document and type whatever you want in your web browser, phone, or tablet: text, bulleted lists, images, and links.

Share a document with others, and give any other Google user "read-only" or full editing access. If they edit your document, you can see both your edits and their edits. You can even roll edits back to a previous state. If you know the right box to check, you can receive an email notification anytime someone else edits that document.

I frequently use Google Docs to journal my tasks. I'll perform repetitive tasks that I want to outsource one day or refine. It could be a task I'll soon forget. I'll document daily activities, but I don't always know what format, or what structure it will fit into, so I use Google Docs for journaling many times. I'll write the date and the tasks I'm thinking about and performing. That gives me research I can refine and clean up later.

Google Sheets (Spreadsheet)

Google Sheets is Google's version of Microsoft Excel that creates and edits spreadsheets (tables) with rows and columns arranged in a grid.

I use Google Sheets to track people I'm contacting for my business. I'll create a column representing the date I added the person to that list, a column for their name, another for their address, and some "notes" about what I want to say to that customer. Then, a checkbox column to mark off that I've contacted that person. (I label the column "Contacted?" and have the cell blank or I type in an "X" if I've contacted them.)

It seems simplistic, but if you must contact 100 people in the next month, if you're a salesman, or customer support representative, you'll need to track your hundreds of repeated activities over time.

Keep it simple and only add columns and rows as you need them. You'll be able to later sort your list by specific columns, or use those "check" columns to track your completions. You track both the future and the past.

Conclusion

Google's free tools are the next iteration of Outlook, Word, and Excel. Gmail gives you control of email again (and you can combine email accounts.) If you already have an existing email account, you can import messages into Gmail to take advantage of labeling, conversations, and archiving. Google Calendar tracks the appointments in your day, and helps you work with others.

These tools synchronize with mobile devices and allow sharing with others. Pop-up notifications appear so you don't miss a thing and you avoid scheduling conflicts because other people see the sub-calendars you grant them access to. Google Drive stores files off-site.

With these productivity tools plus a winning mindset, you're on the path to getting more done, and getting more organized.

As you document your activities, notice the patterns. Notice the templates you could reuse. Use the same document as a starting point for reports. Re-use email templates (canned responses) to save time in the long run.

Important Notes

1. *Gmail* is Google's web based email tool (a replacement for Microsoft Outlook). Its advantages: you can access email anywhere (browser, phone, tablet), it groups conversations together and allows you to use labels and archiving.

2. *Google Calendar* manages your appointments and reminders. You can have sub-calendars and grant others access to view specific calendars, update calendars, or only view if you're free/busy.

3. *Google Drive* is a cloud storage service that you should use to backup important files to the cloud.

4. *Google Sheets* is a spreadsheet tool that's great for tracking progress and repeat tasks.

5. *Drive*, *Docs*, and *Sheets* allow you to share your documents with other Google users (it's free for others to create their own accounts) to varying degrees. For example, you can share a file or folder in Google Drive and make it read-only or writable with others. The same applies with Google Docs and Google Sheets.

Questions

1. What is the difference between messages in your Gmail inbox vs. archived messages that are in *All Mail*?

2. Why is it important to only schedule 3-4 events in your calendar per day?

3. What is a "check column" in Google Sheets?

Chapter 3: Templates & Canned Responses

Have you found yourself typing the same emails or messages to your coworkers, customers, clients, and prospects over and over?

Email Templates

I have a solution for you: use a template. When I create a report (Word document, Google Document, etc.), I don't want to fiddle around with the font face, font size, table of contents, colors, header, and footer. Instead of creating a new document, I frequently copy an old existing document, gut out the inside, and start from scratch.

I'll send emails to people asking, for example, if they want to be guests on my podcast (internet radio show on iTunes). I'll send emails to those same people after they've been on the show to thank them. These are repeat emails I send over and over, but I'll change one sentence or edit their name into the message. I don't want to type five sentences or paragraphs from scratch.

If you had to send 100 emails this week, and if each of those emails took you 3 minutes to write, you'd spend an hour a day JUST writing emails. More realistically, this tedious "repeat task" would probably take up 3-4 hours of every day. Sound familiar? Instead, use templates so that emails only take 5-10 seconds to write. (100 emails x 10 seconds = 17 minutes.) Click a button, an existing email template appears, tweak that message, and send.

If you type the same email message from scratch, you'll forget to mention something from the original template. You'll type in sentences or talking points out of order, and due to boredom, you'll change the message every time, which means more work for you. Do you get tired or aggravated from typing the same things over and over?

A template saves your time and sanity. It gives you a good starting point you can customize, and ensures you don't miss steps. You won't write sentences out of order. Click a button to drop in your email template (officially a "canned response") into Gmail, or use a similar Google Document as a starting point instead of staring at a blank screen.

Canned Responses

What are templates and canned responses? A template can be the look and feel of a document you're about to create. It can be a starting point for a quick email message you're about to send. It might be a webpage or a graphic that you start from an earlier project and you update it for some new project.

It could be a short reusable checklist. I'll setup a website (using a tool called "WordPress") and customize it in about 20 steps. I'll click a button to install WordPress, install specific plug-ins, change the look and feel of the site, tweak settings, add security and make the website run faster. I could grant additional people access to the site. If I tried to keep all those steps in my head, I'd miss steps, I'd do things out of order, and become tired faster, as opposed to stepping through the checklist.

Find a way to apply this in your job as an employee or your business as an entrepreneur. Do you find yourself sending out that same similar form letter asking very similar questions over and over in response to a certain input? Save that message template as a canned response. Even if you plan on customizing that canned response or template later, you can drop in a good starting point, and Gmail can manage all this without you having to juggle different Word documents around.

Warning: when creating lists, checklists (and spreadsheets later in this book), be wary about over-engineering your system. Don't "take a week off" to create 20 checklists and canned responses.

Instead, only create canned responses and templates as you go. I guarantee you'll experience "growing pains" as you transition into a systematized checklist mindset. But don't create 10 to 20 templates "just in case." That only makes the problem worse. You'll spend time managing, organizing, and thinking through this monster you've created. Instead, think about one repetitive email message you send on a regular basis. Keep this in mind throughout the day as you reply to and send emails. Look in your sent folder in Gmail and see if you send the same message on repeat.

You must enable the "canned response" feature in Gmail. After logging in, click the "gear" icon on the top right and choose Settings, then Labs. Where it says *Canned Responses*, choose *Enable* and save.

Go to the compose button and start typing a message. In the bottom right corner, a pop-up appears. Many options are there, but one is for canned responses. Type the initial message as if you're about to send, then save as a canned response, and name it to find it later. The next time you send out a similar message, pull up the canned response, drop it in, and send it as-is or customize it slightly to the specific person that you're replying to.

Canned Responses in the Real World

In my own online business, I wanted to give away a short digital report (PDF document). For people to get that report, I asked them to reply to an email I had sent and answer me a one-word answer.

I wanted people to ask for the report. They had to give me something in return. Hundreds of responses flooded in. If I had to manually type hundreds of replies, I'd never finish. Instead, I created a canned response. In one click, I created a message that said, "Thanks for your response. Here is a link to the report I promised you."

I opened the first email message, clicked Reply, then loaded the proper canned response, and Sent. It took two seconds. I replied to several messages that otherwise would have taken days.

Canned responses are built into Gmail. Create them as you go. Use the compose window to write or reply to emails, and then save them as you need them or load them to get them back.

Take note if some canned responses go unused. You're free to delete them. If you find that you have tons of canned responses, they need organizing. For example, in my own business, I'll create canned responses for websites or projects, and in your own office environment, you might have canned responses meant for coworkers and others meant for customers. You might rename some canned responses so that they begin with the word "coworker" or begin with the word "customer" so you can easily locate them.

Conclusion

Systematize what you do, simplify and get more done in less time, have the option to delegate and know exactly what you're doing. Sit at the computer and complete more in forty minutes than most will get done in an afternoon. If you are working in an office environment and you're someone else's employee, you might not be able to delegate your job, but if you finish a huge chunk of the day in a focused forty-minute session, this takes the pressure off of you trying to catch up or meet those deadlines.

Repeat what works. After you get through the growing pains of what types of emails to write or how to use Google tools, you'll have more fun and you'll have more clarity to focus on the creative side. Systematic processes run in the background for you. You're freed up to think about the bigger picture.

Now you can think, "I need to reply to twenty people. I'll click the canned response." You're not using precious brain power to think of words and sentences that basically say the same thing.

If you need to contact fifty past customers... click, click, click... send those canned responses out. Think in terms of the big picture (those fifty emails as a group) as opposed to fifty paragraphs you have to write.

This avoids the "chipping away" effect that we talked about with to-do lists. Don't chip away and don't suffer through it.

Have fun, be creative, be focused, finish quickly, and complete everything that you start.

Tips & Shortcuts

1. Gmail has a built-in feature called "Send and Archive." When you reply to an email, the default behavior is send your message AND archive the conversation so you can move onto the next one. This saves you a click every time.

2. Tab + space: When I compose an email message, I've trained myself to type the message, and when I'm done, I'll first type the "tab" key on the keyboard, then "space." The "Tab" jumps me out of the composition textbox and to the "Send" button, and the space key on the keyboard pushes the button. This may seem trivial, but this saves precious seconds switching your hands to the mouse over and over.

3. Shift + click: If you need to select a bunch of inbox messages at once (to delete or archive several), use shift + click. Click the box for an email message, hold down the shift key on your keyboard, and then click on a checkbox about 10 messages down. You'll select all 10 messages without having to click 10 times.

Important Questions

1. Why is it so important to use canned responses as opposed to typing a quick email message or "grabbing a template from a text file"?

2. Where in Gmail should you go to enable the canned responses feature?

3. Why is it important to only create canned responses as you go along?

Chapter 4: Follow-Through & Complete Everything You Start

If you feel overwhelmed and frustrated, and you can't crack a specific problem... break that problem down into exactly FOUR manageable chunks.

Minimum Viable Product

If that problem is too big and you can't break it down into four manageable chunks, identify the *minimum viable product*, or the first (rough) draft, the first milestone. The bare minimum effort to have something complete, then break that down into four pieces.

In my own business, I create web pages. I'll create a web page that has a specific background color or color scheme for the text, and a certain font size. I'll drop in a template for that. I need to fill in words for a headline, then explain a problem. I'll describe a membership site, or course, or software product that I then want someone to buy to solve that problem.

That's a huge task. A 20-page long landing page, or sales letter to convince someone to buy seems like a tough nut to crack.

If I'm overwhelmed, I'll dial it back. *What's the shortest or easiest type of landing page or sales letter I can create?* Perhaps half a page of text.

Then I think, what is the barebones *minimum viable product*? I'll create a webpage with a headline, bullet points, and a button to click. Break it down into exactly four pieces. Not three, or ten... four manageable pieces.

- **Milestone One:** Setup the blank webpage or blank template, and that's one step in the right direction.

- **Milestone Two:** Create a button someone can click to buy (a PayPal button) and place it on the bottom of that webpage. That by itself is a way for someone to pay me money.

- **Milestone Three:** I will add one sentence, one headline at the top of that page so that someone knows what they're buying from me.

- **Milestone Four:** I can list a few bullet points so people have more details about what they're buying.

I'm sure you can relate or you can find some similarities to dialing it back to the minimum viable product, and breaking it down into four manageable pieces.

When I worked at a 9-to-5 job as a "web systems administrator", I'd setup computers and servers, and write down or document the things that I did. This involved setting up servers, and I'd type short sentences in a Google document so I wouldn't forget steps. I'd take screenshots of screens and web pages so I could repeat later (hint: Alt + Print Screen on your keyboard, right-click and paste into the Google document, right-click again to Crop, and resize).

If I tried to do all these things at once, I'd be completely overwhelmed. Instead, I broke it up into four pieces. I had a

Google Document open on one computer screen, or one monitor. (By the way, having two monitors for a computer is a huge productivity boost.)

- **Step One:** I'd take screenshots or screengrabs of my browser window, or of the program I had on my screen.

- **Step Two:** After I finished my steps, I'd go back to that document, look at the screenshots, and explain why I typed what I did or clicked where I clicked in that step in the process.

- **Step Three:** List different codes, numbers, or words (but NOT critical passwords) and required tools. That way, if I picked up this task in 6-12 months, or my replacement consulted that document, they could repeat the exact process without my help.

- **Step Four:** I'd make one final pass and list the dangers, or the "don'ts" in addition to those important steps.

Follow-through and complete what you start with this process: problem, milestone, steps, debug, and journal.

Problem

Identify the problem you want to solve. Maybe you're not making enough money for your business, or you can't play basketball, you need to swim, or run faster. Perhaps you need to schedule an appointment for your boss. Figure out what problem this task is solving, that way you can see if the steps you provided solve that problem or not.

Milestone

Instead of shooting for that perfect end goal, decide on a "good enough" milestone. What gets you 80% of the way there to an imperfect but complete (functional) state?

What does "good enough and finished for now" until the next iteration look like? What does version 1.0 or the minimum viable product look like?

Milestone (example)

Here's an example: let's pretend you're a virtual assistant and it's your job to schedule appointments for someone. Create a quick Google Document by going to Google.com/drive, then in the top left corner, click "New" and then "Google Document."

An incoming email arrives from a client asking to get an appointment for your "boss." You'd explain in the Google Document the problem you're solving is that someone needs to meet with your boss. The solution: that appointment is booked on the boss's calendar.

List steps to decide if the meeting goes forward. For example, perhaps they need to pay a coaching fee before they're allowed to book an appointment. You might need to check a Google Calendar for availability. Explain how someone would check that calendar. Do you need view a specific calendar? Email a specific person for approval? Which calendar do you actually add that appointment on, and how can someone quickly check to see if they have access to do that?

Do you need to follow-up via email with a canned response? What milestone gets you almost all the way there?

It won't be perfect. For example, you might have a special case or an unusual request that doesn't quite fit the template, and to account for this "catch-all" scenario, add instructions to forward that email to someone specific or ask a question from someone specific.

Steps

Break it down into steps to get to that milestone. The number "four" is big enough that we can fit all the information in, but it's not so large that we can't keep it in our head. Four steps to get to that milestone.

I'll repeat: chipping away is BAD! Don't think about 100 items when you only need to concern yourself with one or two right now, and complete this task within three days so that you finish it.

Earlier, I gave you the "website creation" example. I'd drive myself CRAZY if I thought too much about those small unimportant pieces. Running spell check, adding images.

Instead, the four steps are: 1. create the webpage itself, 2. create the buttons someone can click on at the bottom, 3. create a headline, and 4. create bullet points.

Preferably, if you can fit a large project into a three-day window with four sittings each of those three days, that's perfect. Three 45-minute sessions and one 10-minute session for each "sitting."

Debug

Things always look perfect on paper. You figured out the problem, the solution, and the steps to get from that problem to the solution, but you're going to need to work out the kinks.

It's one thing to list steps, clicks, and screenshots. You might find yourself going through these steps and realizing that you need to tell someone to check a certain box, avoid a certain screen, or click past a certain page. Programmers call this "debugging" or just "trial and error."

Debug (example)

Example: My goal is to contact people to appear as expert interview guests on my podcast (internet radio show).

I'll make a spreadsheet in Google Drive. Open Google.com/drive, and in the top left corner, click "New" and then "Google Sheets."

I'll add columns as I go, but to start, I'll create a column for the date, and another to represent the name of the person I'm contacting. A column for the email address sounds good, or their contact info such as their Skype address, and possibly one or two other details.

I'll create a "check" column that asks if I've contacted the person. I'll fill this spreadsheet with 10, 20, or 30 people that I will contact in the future. I'll contact these people using Gmail and Canned Responses, then switch back to Google Sheets to check off those items.

Journal

I'll delegate this task in the future, so for now, I create a Google Document explaining these steps to the person performing this task in the future.

I'll say, "Here's the process for going through and researching someone to contact for my podcast." Then, "Here's how I fill up that spreadsheet with people to contact."

Four daily tasks and chunking are super important here. I don't want to switch gears all the time, so I'll fill up this spreadsheet with 10 or 20 or 30 people. If I have a 10-minute or 45-minute session where I contact others using Canned Responses, I'll get a lot done in very little time.

- First, I'll create that spreadsheet containing only the columns I think I need for now (less is more)

- Next, fill that spreadsheet up with people to contact

- Then, step through each row in the spreadsheet. Find that person's contact details, switch to Gmail, drop in a Canned Response, then customize the message with their name and details based on the Google Sheet. Add their email address and their name, and send.

- Finally, check off that cell in the spreadsheet to mark that I've contacted the person.

I'll pick this task up months later, and if I want to outsource this single task in my business, I can hand it off and track that result. The Google Sheet fills up. They can consult with the Google

Document, and Gmail Canned Responses to make the process as idiot-proof as possible.

As you're debugging, journaling is important. A daily activity log of what you're doing, what you're thinking about, and what problems you're solving.

Use short sentences and don't write a novel. List your thoughts and the little tiny hiccups you solved so you don't repeat them. We've all dealt with hiccups, especially when it comes to websites, computers, and software. As an employee or an entrepreneur, setup a Facebook ad that sends traffic to a website. There are many ways to go wrong, and many areas where you'll get stuck like a deer in headlights if you don't know what you're looking at.

Conclusion

Don't worry about making a proper document. List today's date, and type sentences about what you did, what you researched, what you tried, what didn't work, and what did work.

When it comes time to hand that document to someone else, you have a great starting point. Turn those tasks that you thought were "magic" into systems. You're converting yourself (piece-by-piece) from the starving artist with short bursts of productivity (and long periods of burnout) into a machine that functions daily. Plug yourself into the machine and complete those steps, or hand it off to someone else.

Go to a site like Fiverr.com (for one-off jobs), UpWork.com (for hourly jobs), or Rev.com (for transcriptions), and find someone that can handle, out of your 10 tasks, the one task, for example, finding podcast guests. Setting up landing pages. Setting up websites or customizing graphics.

Identify the problem, narrow it down into a milestone, break that milestone up into four steps, repeat with trial and error daily actions, and the spreadsheet, and then keep a daily activity log in a Google Document. That way you know what you did, and you can go back and connect the dots, and reuse that document to create an operations manual for anyone, including you, to pick up later.

Summary & Questions

1. What's the bare minimum (version 1.0) working and complete form of your project that you can publish within the next three days?

2. What are some easy milestones for it? (Then break those milestones down into four manageable pieces.)

3. Problem, milestone, steps, debug, journal.

4. "Chunking" gives you a huge boost in productivity. For example, if you're contacting people (and using a Google Sheet to track it), contact 10 people at a time to avoid wasting time switching gears.

Productivity Boosts

1. On your keyboard, hold down the "Alt" key and hit "PrintScreen" to take a screenshot. Right-click and paste into a Google document, right-click again to crop, then left-click and drag a corner of that cropped screenshot to resize.

2. Use two monitors if you have a bit of technical know-how. In most cases, no additional hardware is required other than that second monitor. Ask a technical person to look, but the back of your computer may have two HDMI (or DVI) ports, and in that case, you'll plug-in that extra monitor for a HUGE workspace. Search "samsung monitor" on Amazon to locate that second monitor for $150.

3. Consider Fiverr.com for outsourcing quick tasks, Upwork.com for hourly tasks, Rev.com for transcription.

Chapter 5: Help Desk & Operations Manual (ZenDesk)

Remove yourself from the day-to-day grind to focus on creative, fun and fulfilling activities. Outsourcing alone is not enough. Are you shy about outsourcing because you're someone else's employee? If you run your own business, have you been burned by outsourcers? Were they expensive, slow, lazy?

Outsourcers do exactly what you tell them to do. If you're unhappy with their output, ask yourself, "Based my instructions, did they fulfill that task?" That way, you know if the problem is with your worker (replace them) or with your system (refine the instructions).

That's a better system and less of a gamble than hiring someone to say, "Make a web page for me. Be my assistant. Get podcast guests." Piece it out into steps and hand it off with simple instructions. That way, you get the exact result you asked for.

We've talked about productivity and mindset, Google tools, and canned responses. Repeat the processes you're building right now to simplify, accelerate, and repeat those tasks. (Run Facebook ads, contact podcast guests, cold call prospects, etc.)

If you're overwhelmed with emails, archive unimportant or "handled" messages. Use labels in conversations and canned responses. If you notice you're constantly juggling customer requests via email, or you're constantly forwarding/replying, it's time to offload some of your communication to a customer help desk, if you haven't already.

ZenDesk Help Desk

When multiple people are involved in your business, it pays to have a help desk. (We recommend *ZenDesk*.) Also, this help desk concept is something you can introduce either to your own single-person entrepreneurial business, or your organization if you are an employee.

A help desk replaces you as the "answerer of emails and requests." A customer opens a ticket instead of sending an email, to describe their problem, issue, or message. They choose which "department" their request belongs to (customer feedback, refund request, feature request, etc.)

In our business, we sell training courses about how to publish podcasts, publish books, run webinars and setup membership sites. We sell software products that create landing pages, membership sites, and others that backup and clone WordPress sites.

We need a way to differentiate between personal email (sent to Robert Plank or my business partner, Lance Tamashiro) as opposed to a general customer service request.

Do you understand the difference between a personal email and a customer service request? A *customer service request* might be that a customer asks for a download link to a thing they bought. They might ask for you to ship something to them, or a refund. They could ask for help with a product.

Someone could send you a *personal email* asking if you can speak at an event, appear on a podcast or sell coaching.

There's difference between email sent to *you* and email sent to *your business*. Business emails should forward to a help desk. This means when someone sends an email to that address, it is instead forwarded to the help desk and automatically opened a ticket.

The sender can go back to that ticket and reply. They see the complete conversation. They see if their ticket is open or closed, if they're still waiting for a response from your or if the matter has been put to bed.

You're no longer hunting around for emails. Customers are no longer yelling at you because you "lost the message" or because they never received your reply. The entire conversation is stored on the "ZenDesk" web-based help desk. A customer opens a ticket and gets a response from you. At any time, you login to the system and see the open tickets. When you want to delegate or outsource, bring more people into this help desk system. Anyone qualified to answer a ticket can reply to it.

A help desk (support desk) is important for systematizing your business by dealing with the incoming messages from customers. You'll see what types of customer requests come in, how they're handled, and which requests take the most time (are the most difficult). Look at your metrics and get a good idea of what customers want, what customers aren't happy about, and this makes you replaceable because help desks have operators. You can be the one operator of the help desk.

A New Employee (Operator) Jumps In

Hire another employee like our employee Jason who then jumps into the help desk from time to time and answers the low-level requests, such as people who want to recover a lost password, or those few people who want refunds.

If you've never seen a help desk before, it might look awkward until you know a few terms. Think of "tickets" as help desk "conversations." In the past, a customer sent you an email, but today, they go to the help desk. They click a button and open a ticket. The form to open a ticket asks for a subject, and asks for their name and email address. The customer types their actual message.

They may be able to specify a category. Which specific product is this for, or what kind of request is this? Is this about a new feature for a software product? Is this a request for a media appearance? Is it a refund request? This way, you can get it to the right person.

If you're still struggling through the growing pain stage of systematizing your business, you can have one day where you deal with only lost password requests, one day where you only deal with refund requests.

You can "machine gun" your replies using canned responses which are built in to most help desk systems! In a ticket system, a "ticket" is the equivalent of an email conversation in Gmail.

A customer opens a ticket. You reply. Other operators can reply. You can enter private notes within that thread. Once the customer's problem is solved, the ticket is marked as "closed."

Departments

Departments are the equivalent of categories, folders, or labels.

For example, we have a software product (Backup Creator) and a software service (Website Remote). Someone can send us a ticket and specify in a drop-down menu if their request relates to the Backup Creator product or the Website Remote product.

They can specify if this is a feature request (which does not need an immediate reply) or a refund request (which requires a faster reply). A department could represent a product, a sub-company of yours, or a type of message such as a refund or feature request.

Operators

When you first create that help desk, you're the only operator, or the administrator. You reply to all messages entered by customers.

Then, you can bring on a business partner or hire an employee. Let's say that new employee's only task for now is to reply to customers who have lost their access to your product. When that type of message comes in, instead of replying to it myself, I'll assign that ticket to an operator named "Jason."

Jason's instructions based on the document I've written for him is the following:

- Login to the help desk

- If there are any tickets assigned to Jason, they will be for lost password requests

- Jason opens a ticket and sees the person's message

- If they gave the adequate amount of information to look it up, then I give Jason the website, and the username, and password to use to login and reset or give that person a new password

- If they did not provide the correct amount of information, Jason should paste in a specified reply. Even better, tell him which canned response to select in the help desk

Tickets

Tickets are the conversation people talk with you about. Departments are the categories. Operators are the people who reply and you can assign tickets to different operators. You can reply using canned responses. You can see the entire conversation with multiple people in the same ticket, and you can have an open ticket, which is like a ticket that's in your inbox where it's still a pressing issue.

You can reply to a ticket which then marks it as pending. This is the middle area. This is a ticket where the issue has not been resolved, but you don't need to see it in the inbox. This is very similar to Gmail's archiving function. A pending ticket still has an open issue but the customer has not yet replied. In many cases, we can set our ticket to automatically close pending tickets after 20 days. If a customer has not replied after 20 days, we will assume the matter is solved, but that customer can always go back in and reopen a ticket. If the ticket is marked as closed, then the customer can then see that we dealt with their issue, and we don't have to see that ticket anymore. We can always go back and find it and read it or even reopen or reply to it, but we have tickets that are open, pending and closed.

How do you transition from your existing system or your existing business into a help desk? First of all, many help desk systems, including ZenDesk, give you instructions on how to setup email forwarding. You can setup a special email account. Our special email account is support@doubleagentmarketing.com. When anyone sends an email message to that address, it creates a new ticket. It creates a new ticket. It marks it as open. It takes the name and email address of the person who emailed you in the first place and sets them as the requester. It places the body of that email message as the body of the ticket itself.

Email Forwarding

If customers aren't used to a ticket system, tell them to email their request into this special email address that forwards into the help desk. That customer sends the email, the help desk receives it and opens a ticket. You only see the new ticket notification, and never the actual email "message." You or an operator can view and reply to that request. This is a great transition tool for you because you've trained people to communicate with you via email, and let's be honest, the average person understands email but not this "ticket" system. Forward customer support emails to that help desk. This creates a ticket and, in some cases, assigns it to the correct operator for a response.

You might be the one and only operator for now, so answer the tickets yourself at first. Why would you do that? Why would you create extra work for yourself? The answer: to see patterns. If you send the same replies to the same types of people, those are canned responses you should create for your help desk (in the same way you created Gmail canned responses.)

Keep a journal of the types of messages you're replying to and the canned responses you're creating. Begin to think about hiring a help desk operator on Fiverr or on Upwork. Upwork is great for hiring someone on an hourly basis because it record periodic screenshots of that worker's computer screen. If someone claims they work for 50 hours but you see they only answered one ticket, you can dispute that based on their screengrabs.

Operations Manual (Top 10 Requests)

Answer your help desk tickets at first to figure out the canned responses to then figure out what operators you need to hire and what instructions to give to them.

Think about the ten types of messages you've replied to. Are some no-brainer messages, are some simple links, or are a few lost passwords? Document the five steps it takes to reset a customer's password and reply to that person. That's one boring task you can outsource to one person for this one job. Use this outsourcer to help to categorize or filter out the things you need to handle.

Think of yourself as the "catch-all" at the top of the food chain.

You'll see different requests coming into your help desk. You hire that person to only handle lost passwords. If a request comes in and based on the text, if they can infer that a customer is asking for a lost password and there is not enough information, you say, "Here's the response." If there is enough information, then here is the action to take, plus the response. If the request that comes in is not this specific lost password task, that help desk operator assigns the ticket to you so you can handle it.

For example, let's say you're not ready to hand out access to grant refunds to people. Have this new employee handle lost passwords only, but if a refund request comes in, they pass it up the food chain to you.

Once you trust this outsourcer, write that journal entry to explain the process to look up a customer, to see if a customer deserves a refund, to grant a customer a refund, and tell them you provided the refund.

Once you have those steps in place, that becomes a second task that outsourcer can handle. If a customer opens a ticket regarding a lost password or a refund request, the employee handles that and passes all other tasks up the food chain to you.

Start an outsourcer with only one task, then slowly add more tasks as you go. This way, your business grows at the pace you want. If that outsourcer becomes too overworked, hire a second worker and tell them how to accomplish one of the offloaded tasks.

Recap

Add operators to your ZenDesk help desk system. If you hire someone new, hire them as a new operator to track them. You can control what they have access to. If you stop paying them, delete their account and revoke their access so they no longer have the keys to the castle.

Forward customer support emails to a help desk. This is superior to email because you have departments, canned responses, and operators. Keep a daily journal to document the patterns. If there's a repetitive task you want to offload, identify the "if-then" steps to solve the problem. If a customer sends in a "lost password" request and they don't give us enough information, reply with a certain response. If they give us the info we need, take the appropriate action.

Apply this to new tasks. Write the "if-then" statements in your journal, meaning the the course of action that someone should take. This includes: marking a ticket as "solved", moving it to a different department or assigning it to a particular operator. That operator might be you, personally!

You could add instructions for someone to lookup information in a database or a CRM system, or they might need to send an email or make a phone call. Include those instructions, including the exact phone number in that operations manual that you write in Google Documents, based on your journal. Later, cleanup these step-by-step "if-then" instructions with screenshots. Anyone should be able to pick up single task for you.

Summary

1. A help desk ticket is a request from a customer. It can be open (not yet handled), pending (waiting on a response from a customer), closed (resolved). You can assign it to a specific operator (person responding to the customer) and to a department (refunds, testimonials, specific products).

2. Operators are people who run your help desk, view tickets, and respond to customers. At first, you're the only operator, but you can add an assistant as a new operator to handle new queries. As you trust that worker more, or perhaps you add multiple workers, you can phase yourself out of the "customer support" aspect of the business. Or at the very least, only respond to special cases.

3. If you or your customers are having difficulty adjusting to the new help desk system, email forwarding is the answer. You can tell customers to email a specific email address (ours is support@doubleagentmarketing.com) or you can forward email requests to your forwarding address to automatically create a ticket based on the incoming email request.

Questions

1. Why is it better to use a help desk system to respond to customers instead of email?

2. Which help desk service do we recommend?

3. What is *Upwork* and what is the advantage to using that service to hiring help desk operators?

Chapter 6: Appointment Scheduler (Calendly)

Do you have "slow days" where nothing gets done? Where did your the time go?

The fix is to have an appointment-based business. I'll sit at the computer to perform a task, in one sitting, on a schedule.

We have coaching clients that we meet with one-on-one for one hour per week. If we didn't have a set time for the day of the week and time of day, and if we didn't have it on a calendar to always notify us, we wouldn't take it seriously, and we wouldn't stick to a set schedule.

So far in *The Checklist Mindset*, we've discussed productivity strategies along with Gmail, canned responses, Google Docs, and ZenDesk. I'm assuming that you're using many of these tools at the same time for maximum effect.

Out of everything so far, that online calendar is my favorite. Google Calendar allows you to stick to important meetings and knock out tasks in a focused periods of time, short bursts of productivity, so you aren't stuck on the computer all day.

Appointment-Based Business

According to my online calendar, I met with my business partner at 9AM on Monday, in the Pacific time zone. I interviewed a podcast guest (a podcast is an internet radio show on iTunes) from 12PM to 12:30PM, and another from 1PM to 1:30PM. I completed other tasks that day, but those were my pressing appointments.

- On Tuesday, I streamed a video message on Facebook from 11AM to 12PM

- On Wednesday, I met with a coaching client from 11AM to 12PM

- On Thursday, I met with two additional coaching clients

- On Friday, I interviewed three separate guests to create three additional podcast episodes

Showing up to one meeting after another is easy. I can check my meetings in the morning. I need to be at the computer for these specific points in time, and when I'm done, I'll walk away from the computer.

There are many situations where you'll want to provide "office hours" in one form or another. I interview many people for my podcast, but I don't want someone to schedule themselves on a Friday night or a Sunday morning.

I want to restrict those office hours to specific days and hours, like Monday and Friday mornings from 10AM to 12PM, but I want podcast guests to be able to choose ANY Monday or Friday coming up, excluding holidays and days off, and possibly select a specific time slot within those ranges. For example, Monday three weeks from now from 11:30AM to 12:00PM.

I also want to collect contact information when someone books an appointment with me, such as a phone number or Skype username.

The appointment scheduler Calendly, located at Calendly.com, connects to Google Calendar. Set these office hours. (Calendly calls these "activities.") Give a prospect or client a special link to schedule themselves for that "activity." After that choose a time slot and enter their details, that time is blocked out, and you see it on your any sub-calendar of Google Calendar that you choose. You're notified, and anyone else with access to that sub-calendar sees that you have an appointment at that time.

This takes out the guesswork. Show up at the time you're supposed to, complete the task and it's done.

Scheduler Case Study

I use Calendly to schedule one-off coaching meetings (40 minutes on Tuesdays) in addition to meeting with podcast guests. This 40-minute coaching call "activity" is different than the 20-minte podcast interview "activity." We keep the link private, and if someone pays us money, they get access to the link, where they can schedule themselves. They choose a date and select a specific time slot to reserve that time on that date. They enter their name and email address, and a phone number or Skype username.

You need an online scheduler for your appointments to avoid the back and forth of scheduling. Have you ever tried scheduling an appointment with someone without a scheduler? It's terrible:

- You say, "I need to meet with you. Or you need to meet with me, so let's figure out a date."

- They say, "I have Monday, Wednesday, and Friday open." You ask, "How about Wednesday?"

- They respond, "What time Wednesday?"

- You say, "I have 7:00 AM to 12:00 PM open."

- They respond, "I don't have that time available. Can you do the afternoon?"

- You say, "Sure, let's do 2:00 PM to 2:30 PM." You ask, "What time zone?"

- They reply, "Eastern time zone, GMT minus 5 hours."

- Then you say, "I've scheduled an appointment."

- You reply, "Here are the details for our appointment."

The above scenario required 9 instances of back-and-forth email replies, and could take weeks. We're not even getting into cancellations and rescheduling issues.

Calendly's scheduler avoids this back-and-forth and avoids the time zone headache. It shows available appointments in your, and your prospect's, respective time zones.

The client looking to schedule office hours can click around and see your available appointments without having to guess or try different days of the week or different times.

They choose a time slot and schedule themselves in their own time zone. The appointment shows up in your Google Calendar in your own time zone.

It looks for conflicts. If you tell me you can meet for a podcast interview on Monday or Friday, but I have something already scheduled at noon, Calendly doesn't make that time slot available to you.

Google Calendar synchronizes with any other device, so you can use it on a computer, laptop, tablet or phone and share with anyone you want.

You define the office hours and the rules. You can say that you only can meet with someone on Tuesdays from 8AM to 12PM your time, and it adjusts for the time zone. You can say that they can schedule a meeting with you in thirty-minute or one-hour blocks. You can specify that you will only take two meetings per day: if two people schedule for that day, no other slots will be available.

You can specify that people need to schedule an appointment one week ahead of time. You can block out a range of dates. You can setup any rules and restrictions for these office hours to ensure that people can't blindly add appointments to your calendar.

The calendar connection between Calendly and Google Calendar is important because it can look at multiple calendars and say, "If there's family time, clients cannot book a spot during that time. If there is an existing interview, they cannot book a spot. If I have a special meeting, they cannot book a spot, but if a colleague has his (or her) own meeting, unrelated to me, ignore that specific sub-calendar.

Organize your life with an online scheduler. Think of it like a teacher or a college professor's open hours to ask you anything. Have a set block of open hours where anyone can ask you anything.

You can still use Calendly if you're an employee and you want to make yourself available to meet with other co-workers or prospects, but you don't want them to drop in at any time.

I've used Calendly many times for podcast interviews and it replaces many tasks that formerly required a personal assistant.

Use Calendly and hook it up to your Google Calendar. Now that you're using an online scheduler along with these different productivity and Google tools, repeat and scale up. Look at more things you can remove from your business to get the same result as opposed to adding more complexity.

Repetitions. Fill up that calendar. If you run a podcast show, wouldn't it be great to consistently have one or two guests completely scheduled every day? If you're looking for website traffic, how great would it be to show up to meetings? This also applies to sales calls and everything in between.

Have an appointment-based business and make the best use of your hour. Are you doing measly $5-an-hour work? Or, are you doing $100-an-hour work (or more) because you've used outsourcing and the tools to avoid the time creep?

Use these tools and automate as much of your business as possible if your business is something that you own or if you're an employee for someone else.

Key Takeaways

1. Signup with Calendly and connect it to your Google Calendar to provide office hours for client demos, coaching calls, media interviews, and more.

2. Define an activity (for example, a "20 minute coaching call" or "40 minute media interview") within Calendly and set rules (i.e. what days of the week and times during those days) as well as restrictions (no more than 2 appointments per day, or appointments must be made a week in advance).

3. After your Calendly account, activities, Google Calendar connection, rules and restrictions are setup, hand out a special link via email or a secret web page, such as a membership site.

Important Questions

1. What is an appointment based business?

2. Why is an online scheduler such as Calendly so important to save time scheduling meetings?

3. What does Calendly give you that sharing a Google Calendar with a co-worker does not?

Chapter 7: Automation Triggers (Zapier)

It's important that the tools you use to increase your productivity don't use you. Machines can do most of your work for you.

If you're looking to lighten your own load as an employee, there are many tools that simplify your important tasks. If you're an overworked, overwhelmed business owner who thought that creating your own income was the secret to your financial freedom and you accidentally created a second job for yourself, plug these automatic tools to do these things for you.

Example #1: you can monitor a specific YouTube user's channel, and if that particular user uploads a new video, you can have a blog post appear that posts that same YouTube video within minutes of posting, completely hands free.

Additionally, once that blog post goes live, that link can automatically appear on your social media channels (Facebook and Twitter) to send traffic back to that blog post where you placed someone else's YouTube video on your site.

My favorite automation tool for this purpose is called Zapier.com and it runs on "triggers." A new piece of content is posted on a site, and Zapier re-posts it somewhere else, such as your own blog, social media, or even a CRM or Google Spreadsheet.

Example #2: When you post something on one of your Facebook fan pages, Zapier can replicate the post on your own Facebook timeline or on other fan pages.

Example #3: When someone schedules an appointment with you (a podcast interview, for example), and it appears on your Google calendar, it's also copied over to a special Google spreadsheet.

Example #4: If a very important email comes from a specific email address or has specific keywords, it can call your telephone and tell you to run to your computer and check it.

Workflow automation tools like these save you busy work. You don't have to hire an assistant that a tool can do 24 hours a day.

Zapier Automation Explained

Zapier monitors triggers, and triggers take different actions. For example, if someone purchases something from you on a Shopify store, it can send a text to your phone. If the weather in your area every morning is between a certain temperature range (or if it's going to rain), Zapier can ping a webpage, send an email, or make a phone call.

If someone signs up for a GoToWebinar session, Zapier can add that person to an Aweber or MailChimp mailing list.

Every time someone mentions you on Twitter, Zapier can add that tweet as a row in a special Google Spreadsheet.

Zapier can monitor different blogs or YouTube channels for specific keywords. Perhaps it monitors 50 websites for three or four specific keywords, and aggregates or re-blogs all that content onto a single site.

If someone wants to be a guest on my show, they'll first send me an email with some details. If I approve, I'll reply with a canned response saying, "Here are your steps and here's what you need to know. Here's the link to my Calendly scheduler." They click on that link, they find a time slot that works best for them, and after they fill in that time slot and give me the information about that appointment, I get an email from Calendly. I also get a message on my Google calendar.

Zapier also monitors my Calendly appointments and adds a new row in a special Google spreadsheet containing: date of the appointment, the person's name, their email address, and their Skype address so I can call them to record the interview. I only have to show up when the calendar appointment tells me!

Not only is this spreadsheet auto-populated as the appointments fill up, I can edit the spreadsheet afterwards for follow-ups. I've added additional "check columns" in that spreadsheet. I can mark an "X" in a cell to indicated if I've interviewed that person. Another columns represents whether or not I've published the recording online. Yet another shows I've thanked a guest for appearing on the show. Another, whether or not I've promoted the show on Twitter. Zapier fills in the rows for me and leaves a few columns blank. I fill in the rest as I work my way down in those rows.

I also use Zapier to copy blog posts to social media. I have a blog at RobertPlank.com where my podcast episodes appear, along with text-based and video-based posts.

Zapier monitors that site. If I make a new post on that website, it automatically posts about it on my "Robert Plank Show" fan page. It links to the webpage and adds a picture with a short description.

I also use Zapier to replicate posts from The "Robert Plank Show" fan page to our "Double Agent Marketing" fan page and to my Facebook timeline.

Trigger Stacking

You can stack multiple triggers. I record a new podcast episode and post it on my blog. It's copied to my fan page. That post is copied to my other fan page. That post is also copied to my personal Facebook timeline.

I've setup Zapier to monitor my business partner's website at LanceTamashiro.com. If post a new blog entry or podcast episode, that link appears on my fan page within minutes. Once again, that fan page post is copied to my Facebook timeline and other pages hands-free.

I also use Zapier to monitor my own YouTube channel and to monitor Lance's YouTube channel.

- When I post a new video, I only need to upload it to YouTube.

- Zapier sees that new video and posts it as a post on my blog.

- Zapier sees a new blog posts and posts it to my Robert Plank Show fan page.

- Zapier sees that new post on the Robert Plank Show fan page and also posts that on the Double Agent Marketing fan page.

- Zapier sees the Double Agent Marketing posts and also makes a post on my personal Facebook timeline.

I could set it up to automatically post to Twitter and so on.

Using Zapier, I could setup a Gmail "filter" so that any incoming email matching specific keywords could forward to a special Zapier email address and call or text me to let me know that this urgent email has arrived.

Create an account at Zapier.com and choose which tools to connect together, for example:

- YouTube plus WordPress if you want a new YouTube video to appear on your WordPress blog.

- WordPress plus Facebook if you want a new blog post on your WordPress site to then appear on Facebook.

Triggers

The trigger sets off everything. If I wanted YouTube to cause an action, the trigger is YouTube. Go through a simple step-by-step process and say, "Here's the YouTube channel to monitor. If this YouTube channel adds a new video, perform this action. Post to WordPress." I can make another trigger based on my WordPress blog and say, "Anything posted on my WordPress blog goes to my Facebook page."

As part of the trigger setup process, Zapier's step-by-step screens might ask for a web address or even a login to a specific site.

Actions

An action is what Zapier does with that information given by the trigger.

Zapier gives me the "fields" such as the video title, link to the video, the description of the video, and so on. If a new YouTube video was posted, I could take the title of the video and make that the title of a blog post on WordPress. I could make the video code itself be the body of the blog post in WordPress. If the video has a description, I could put the description of that at the top and so on. Connect these systems and decide which fields from the trigger match up to which fields in the action.

This even applies to a Google spreadsheet. If someone uploads a new YouTube video, Zapier could take the title and plug it into a specific column in a new row of a Google spreadsheet. It could take the link to the video and plug it into the corresponding column in that new Google spreadsheet row.

Because it's a Google spreadsheet, I choose to share it with someone else who has a Google account. They can set it up to receive notifications when a new row is added onto that spreadsheet.

What does this mean? I could hire a virtual assistant to do research and monitor new videos from specific channels or with specific keywords. That assistant could watch those videos and take notes for me, or click the "like" button on those videos for me. Zapier populates a spreadsheet and the outsourced worker only has to "clock hours" when there's some new action to be performed.

Filters

I don't want to get too advanced with you, but Zapier can become even more powerful if you use filters.

Let's say that you decided that you wanted to create a blog about the latest Apple products (iPhones, iPads, Apple Watches, Apple TVs, and so on.)

You could manually follow the top tech blogs and top YouTube channels that talk about Android phones and Microsoft tablets, such as ArsTechnica, TechCrunch, and Gizmodo.

Instead, tell Zapier to monitor these popular websites and YouTube channels. These sites could post 20-30 every day, but you tell Zapier (using filter) to only take action if the word "Apple" is in the title of the article, or it contains words like iPhone or iPad in the title of the videos and posts. Then, only take action (filling in a spreadsheet, re-posting) on that small subset of articles.

Back to trigger stacking, you could setup other triggers to replicate the content on your site to other social media channels.

Filters are optional, but be aware that you can combine triggers (that set things off), filters (choose if this particular trigger should fire based on criteria), and actions (apply the information from those triggers into new content).

Conclusion & Analysis

I strongly believe that the tools and techniques we've discussed apply to you regardless of your skill level, and apply to you whether you're a self-employed work-at-home entrepreneur or an employee for someone else.

- *Zapier* allows you to connect different tools together, such as YouTube, WordPress, Facebook, Twitter, Google Sheets, and even phone calls and SMS text messages.

- *Calendly* makes it easy to set "office hours" and flexible appointments.

- A *ZenDesk* help desk gives you a central location to handle customer inquiries.

- *Google Drive* is a free service that stores your files, but its real power is in Google Docs (an online Microsoft Word clone, great for journaling) and Google Sheets (an online spreadsheet program). Edit your files from any device and share with others.

- *Google Calendar* is a place to manage your schedule. It synchronizes with all your devices and you can grant others full or partial viewing access of your appointments.

- *Gmail* is a web-based email program that has several unique features including labels, conversations, and canned resposnes.

Don't use these tools aimlessly. Choose a real goal, such as to increase your social reach, get more traffic, make more sales, build a bigger list. If you're an employee, perhaps your goal is to simply get out of overwhelm, and to simplify.

Find out what you want and use these tools to make your daily life easier, take yourself out of the equation as much as possible, repeat and repeat, then reassess later and course correct.

Transition into the *Checklist Mindset* way of thinking as soon as possible. Hire people to use these tools. They'll look at your help desk, emails, and appointments to take actions. You'll focus on what's most important. Your business (and life) will become fun, profitable, and fast again. You can focus on what matters in life.

Important Ideas

- Zapier is an automation tool that connections website actions together. For example, it can replicate your social media posts across pages or auto-blog YouTube videos. It uses triggers, filters, and actions.

- Triggers are events that happen on the internet, such as: a specific user posted a new video.

- Filters let you set criteria, for example, only continue if that YouTube video has the word "iPad" in it.

- Actions are the things that occur as a result of your action. For example, post a new WordPress blog entry or add a row in a Google Sheet. You'll provide Zapier with any login information and possibly plug "form fields" from your trigger, into your action.

About Robert Plank

Robert Plank creates information products, software tools, and webinar training.

He can show you how to not only save time in your business and everyday life, but do more in less time. Master WordPress. Build your list. Create passive income from information products. Generate residual income using membership sites. Scale and talk to use audiences using webinars. And more!

Robert's Online Presence:

- Blog: www.robertplank.com
- Podcast: www.robertplankshow.com/itunes
- Facebook Page: www.robertplankshow.com

Robert Plank's other titles on Amazon.com:

- 100 Time Savers: Start Less, Finish More, and Cut 10 Minutes a Day from Your Schedule to Gain 60 Hours of Free Time Per Year
- Article Crash Course: Get Published, Get Instant Authority and Become an Expert in Any Subject
- Double Agent Marketing: Live the Double Life, Control Your Destiny and Become a Self-Employed Entrepreneur By Starting Your Own Home-Based Internet Information Business
- Four Daily Tasks: Overcome All Internal Roadblocks Using a Few Simple Rules, Solve Any Personal Problems

and Keep Moving in a "Forward" Direction in 10 Easy Steps
- Internet Marketing on Crack: Master Your Time Management, Marketing, Sales, Traffic, Products, Customer Relationships & More From Just a Few Simple Breakthroughs
- List, Traffic & Offers: The Internet Marketing Profit Shortcut
- Membership Cube: How to Create a Passive Income in Just a Few Simple Clicks
- Secret Conversations with Internet Millionaires: How to Make Money Online with an Internet Marketing Business
- Sell on Amazon FBA: Easy Steps to Create an Online Passive Income Amazon Business with Retail Arbitrage & Private Label Sourcing
- Setup a Point & Click Website Today: Install WordPress, Create Massive Content, Secure and Backup Your Blog WITHOUT Being a Computer Geek

Double Agent Marketing software:

- Website Remote: manage WordPress sites from one place
- Backup Creator: backup and clone WordPress sites
- Paper Template: create landing pages with WordPress
- Member Genius: run a membership site in WordPress

Double Agent Marketing courses:

- Membership Cube: setup a recurring membership site
- Income Machine: establish your online system including your blog, traffic, opt-in page, autoresponder sequence and more
- Dropship CEO: sell physical products on Amazon.com
- Make a Product: self-publish a book (physical and digital) on Amazon.com
- Profit Dashboard: earn money from Fiverr
- Podcast Crusher: create your own podcast

Discover more about him at RobertPlank.com/about and contact him at RobertPlank.com/ask if you have a personal question, want to appear on his podcast, want him on your podcast, or if you wish to enquire about availability for speaking engagements.

Thanks for Supporting the Book

I would like to thank these following people for believing in me:

Alfred McComber, Alun Richards, Anita Cohen, Carlo Selorio, Carole Lawrence, Dale Maxwell, Daryl Thompson, Dianne M. Daniels, Diran Afarian, Donna Kim-Brand, Hanns Paul, Irene Edwards, Jack Joseph, Janis Miller, Jason Wally Waldron, JP Bersier, Kate Mylett, Kenneth Sapp, Kevin Iggins, Lee Booker, Lorenzo Rothery, Martin Hirsch, Marty Richardson, Miguel de Jesus, Phil Johncock, Rick Robert Van Horn, Roger Easlick, Ronald Perry Sr., Scott Buendia, Scott Earley, Tim Jensen, Tony Prodger, Ty Bohannon, Vernon Jeter, Walter Monteiro, and William Holland, William McPeck.

Made in the USA
Middletown, DE
04 June 2020

95672416R00036